Oh No! A Puppy In The House
A Stanley and Albert Tale

Written by Cameron Shamis
Illustrated by Bianca Silva

Copyright © 2022 Cameron Shamis
All rights reserved.
ISBN: 9798218012120

This book is dedicated to my family and friends who now have children and families of their own. This is the first of many books I will have the pleasure of passing along. Stanley, Albert, and I hope you enjoy the story and wish all of you well.

Stanley had spent years training his human to do things at the right times. 5am was first breakfast, then outside time for Stanley to stretch his legs. His human was free to do what he liked until second breakfast at 9am.

After that, Stanley liked to play with his human, teaching him new tricks and making sure he understood that Stanley was the boss. For example, if Stanley wanted to sit on the printer, then that was where Stanley was going to sit!

Sometimes his human went out, which Stanley didn't understand, but he did come back with important things like food, so Stanley allowed it.

When Stanley was a kitten, he liked to run around the house at night and see how often he could get his human out of bed. He looked very funny in his pajamas creeping down the stairs to see if there were burglars!

But Stanley loved his human very much, and soon learned that it was much better to get cuddles all night instead.

Stanley was very stunning when he wanted to be, with a sleek face and fluffy fur around his shoulders. It made him look like a warrior, especially when he teamed it with his 'how dare you?' look. His human was well-trained, so Stanley didn't need The Look much anymore, but he still practiced in front of the mirror. Just in case.

He was doing it now, practicing closing his eyes until they were just right: with a touch of outrage. Perfect. Stanley heard his human coming home. He had been out again.

"Mrrm?" That meant 'What do you have there in that box, human?'

"I've got a surprise for you," said the human. "Come and see!"

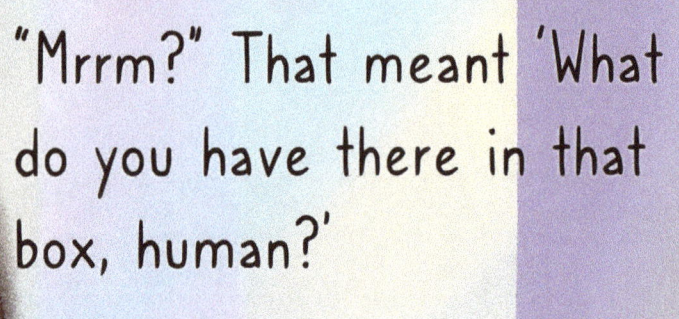

Stanley jumped down and trotted over to the box, hoping that it would be something good to eat. Or something soft to sleep on. Or maybe—

Wait. What was that smell? Stanley stopped. His nose twitched and wiggled. It couldn't be...

"Grhhmm," grumbled Stanley.

But his human didn't listen! He carried on opening the box.

"Hello, little fella!" his human whispered to something inside the box.

Stanley backed off, his ears flat with suspicion. What was this?

The human reached in and gently lifted out a little puppy.

"This is Albert!" said the human. "I wanted you to have a friend, Stanley."

The human had brought a dog into his—Stanley's—house? This was unacceptable! Stanley glared at the wriggling, licking, squirming puppy (really, do dogs have no dignity?) and his human who had allowed this terrible thing to happen.

Albert was making happy noises, yipping and licking the human's fingers and face and—well, just about anywhere he could reach!

Stanley meowed, a cold, cross meow, hoping that would make them understand that he was not happy.

All it did was attract the attention of Albert, who ran over, his long pink tongue flopping and flapping. "Grrrm!" said Stanley. That meant 'Stop!' But Albert did not stop. He ran straight at Stanley and licked his face!

Stanley was so shocked that he froze in horror! Albert licked him again.

"Mewp!" was all Stanley managed to say. He had meant to growl fiercely, but it didn't come out right. The human was sitting on his heels, smiling.

Stanley tried The Look on his human, but it did no good. Albert tried to lick Stanley again. "Mryeowl!" said Stanley. That meant 'No, stay away!' Stanley turned and ran. He wanted to hide and sleep on the human's bed until he felt better.

But Albert followed him! Stanley ran faster, and the puppy ran faster too.

They ran all around the house! Into the kitchen and out the back door, around to the front door and, through the cat flap, up the stairs and down again, into the living room and—there! Stanley's cat tree!

Stanley took a giant leap and landed on the top platform. The whole cat tree swayed, backward and forward, and Stanley had to dig his claws in to stop himself from falling off.

Albert was at the bottom, looking for a way up. He couldn't find one. He sat down and howled a little. "Aroooowl!"

Stanley understood him! It meant 'My new friend is gone and I am sad!'

Stanley was the puppy' friend? Hmm. This needed thinking about.

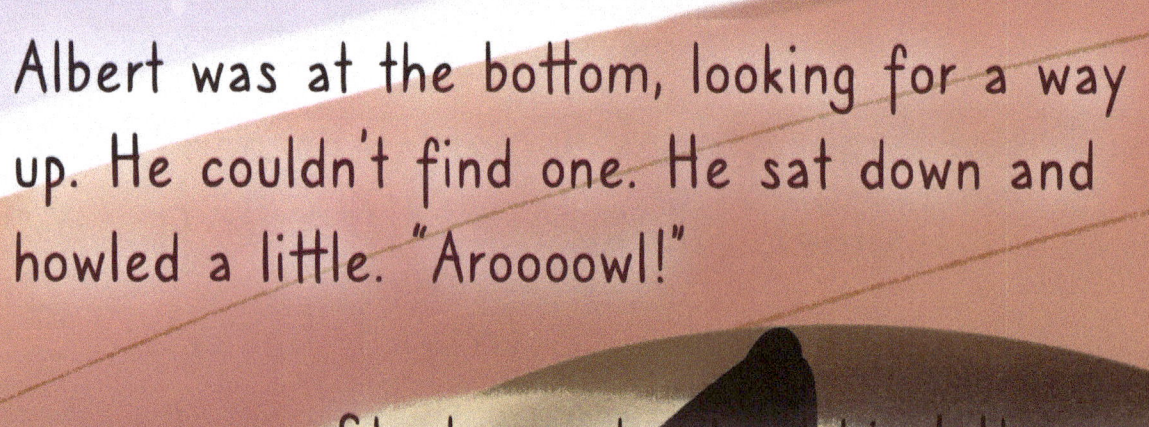

Stanley sat down and began to wash himself—which is something cats do when they are thinking. He washed his face and ears, and made sure his thick coat was beautifully fluffed out.

Thinking and washing took a long time. Albert yawned, showing white little puppy teeth. At one point, he looked at Stanley and tried to copy his movements, but fell over when he couldn't quite get into the right position.

Stanley finished washing and looked down at the pup. Albert yawned again. Then, he curled up on a corner of the carpet and fell fast asleep!

Stanley carefully came down from his high perch and tiptoed over.

He sniffed him carefully from nose to tail. Albert was having a dream. His feet twitched as though he were running. Then he whimpered a little bit.

"Aw," said the human. "He's missing his brothers and sisters, maybe?"

Stanley sat down and gave his human The Look.

"Food time, right, Stanley?" said the human. He went to the kitchen to start making Stanley's lunch.

Albert whimpered again. Stanley went a bit closer. The puppy was nice and warm. Stanley leaned even closer, rubbing his face against Albert's side.

Albert made a happy sound and rolled toward Stanley. They curled up together and napped while Stanley waited for his food to be ready. When the human called, Stanley jumped up quickly.

He wasn't going to let the human know that he quite liked the puppy now, was he?

He ran into the kitchen, meowing hungrily, and nearly got trampled as the puppy came galloping after him.

"You're awake!" said Stanley.

"Yes, friend!" said Albert. "I'm hungry!"

That was all right then, Stanley supposed. He didn't have to share his food. Perhaps it would be okay to share the house with the puppy after all.

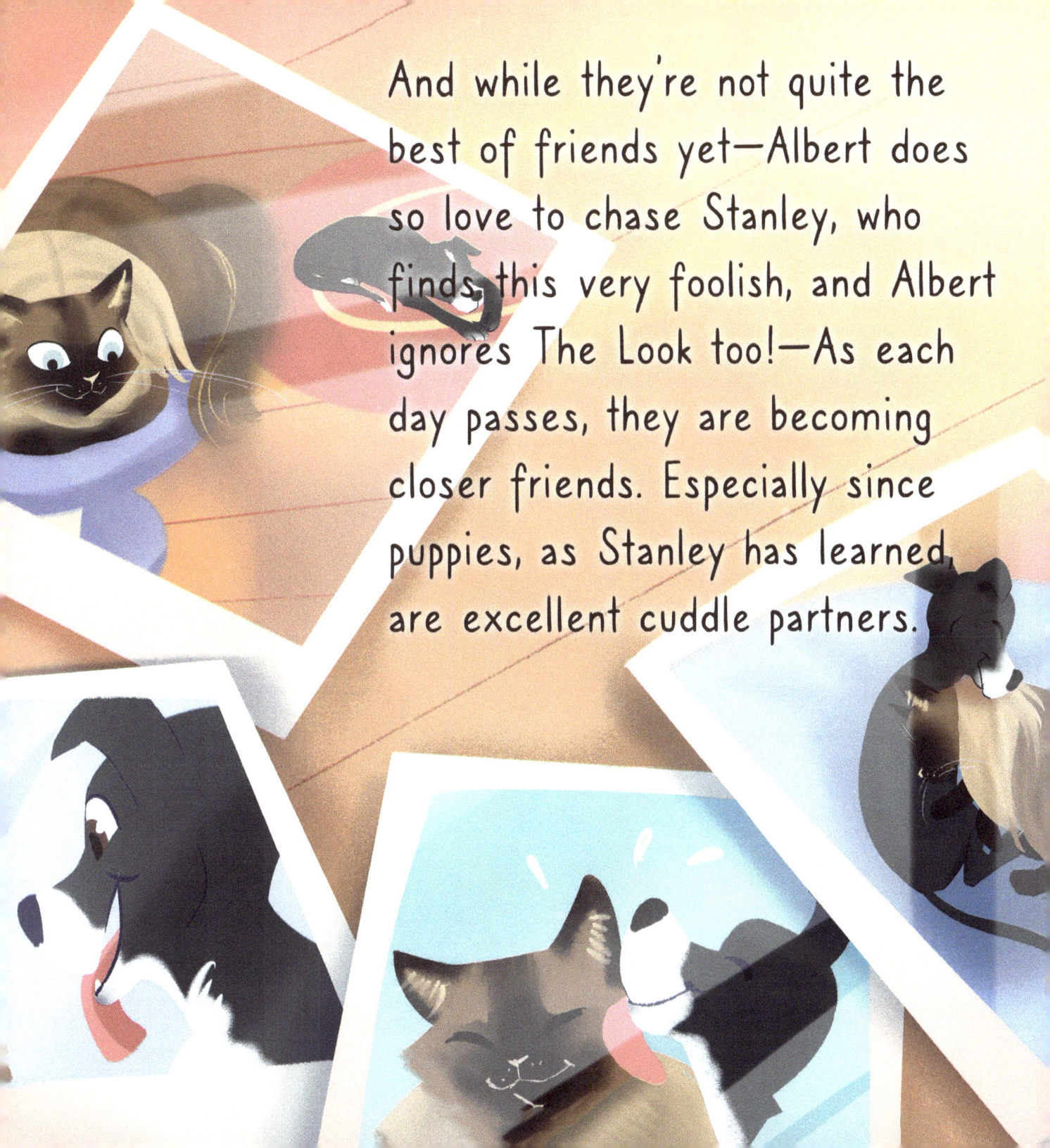

And while they're not quite the best of friends yet—Albert does so love to chase Stanley, who finds this very foolish, and Albert ignores The Look too!—As each day passes, they are becoming closer friends. Especially since puppies, as Stanley has learned, are excellent cuddle partners.

www.ingramcontent.com/pod-product-compliance
Lightning Source LLC
Chambersburg PA
CBHW061356010526
44107CB00012B/947